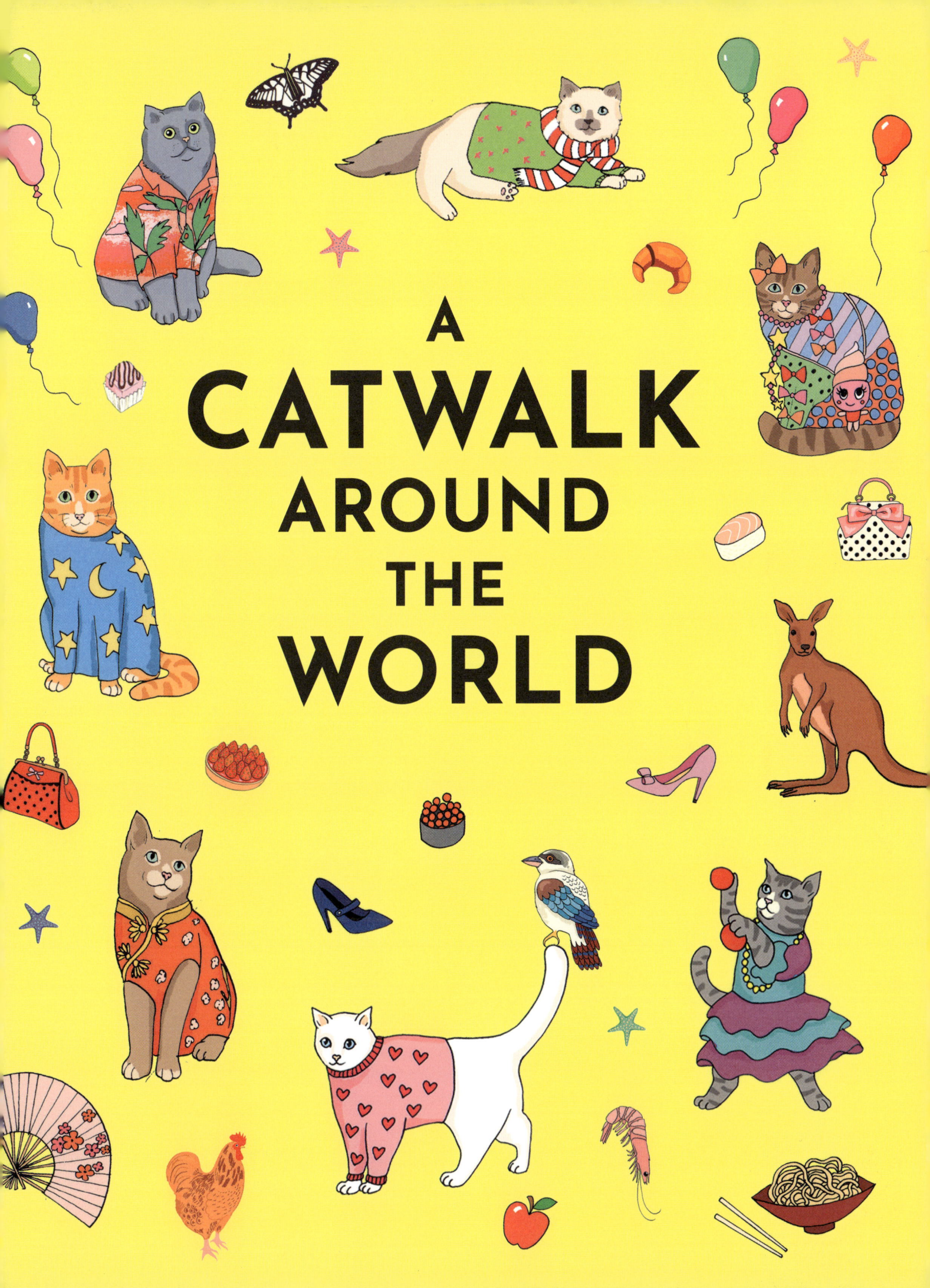

For my darling
daughter, Vivian. xxx

K.M.

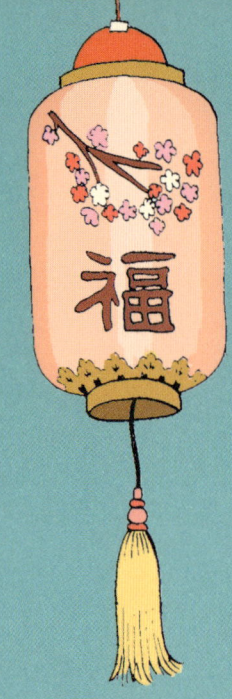

LAURENCE KING

First published in Great Britain in 2025
by Laurence King

Text copyright © Hodder and Stoughton Ltd, 2025
Illustrations copyright © Karen Mabon, 2025

Karen Mabon has asserted her right under the Copyright, Designs
and Patents Act 1988, to be identified as the illustrator of this work.

All rights reserved. A CIP catalogue record for this book
is available from the British Library.

HB ISBN: 978-1-510-23110-8

10 9 8 7 6 5 4 3 2 1

Printed in China

MIX
Paper | Supporting
responsible forestry
FSC® C104740

Laurence King
An imprint of
Hachette Children's Group
Part of Hodder and Stoughton
Carmelite House
50 Victoria Embankment
London EC4Y 0DZ

An Hachette UK Company
www.hachette.co.uk
www.hachettechildrens.co.uk
www.laurenceking.com

The authorised representative in the EEA is Hachette Ireland,
8 Castlecourt Centre, Dublin 15, D15 XTP3, Ireland (email: info@hbgi.ie)

It's a glorious sunny day in the **Scottish Highlands**, home to **Vivian** the cat. Anticipation is in the air as the cats are getting ready for Burns' Night, but Vivian is excited for another reason — she's travelling the world, and you're invited to join her!

1. These cats are wearing bonnie wee clothes. Which of these traditional Scottish items of clothing can you spot the most of?

   Kilt   Tweed   Tam o' Shanter cap

2. Your stomach is rumbling; you're hungry for Scottish cuisine. How many different Scottish delicacies can you spot?

The Scottish Highlands

With lots of wildlife, rolling hills and crystal-clear lakes, the Scottish Highlands are a nature lover's dream!

Kilts

A kilt is a wrap-around piece of clothing made of wool, with heavy pleats at the sides and back and traditionally a tartan pattern. It's not quite a skirt, though they look very similar! They're usually worn with a sporran, which is a small bag traditionally made from leather and fur.

Haggis

Haggis is a traditional Scottish dish made from a sheep's offal, which is the edible internal parts of an animal like the kidney and liver. It's mixed with suet (animal fat), oats and seasonings. Then it's boiled in a bag, traditionally one made from the animal's stomach! Sounds questionable, but if you serve it with neeps and tatties (turnips and potatoes) you're in for a truly tasty feast!

Loch Ness Monster

Also known as 'Nessie', the Loch Ness Monster is an enormous creature in Scottish folklore that is believed to live in the depths of Loch Ness. Do you think Nessie is real?

Burns' Night

Burns' Night is an evening of celebrations held in honour of the Scottish poet, Robert Burns. Held on or around 25 January, Burns' birthday, the event can be celebrated by eating some haggis, reading Burns' poetry and laughing and dancing. It's a great night to party!

Paris and Milan

Paris and Milan are two of the Big Four fashion capitals of the world, along with London and New York City. No wonder all the cats there are so stylish!

La Tour Eiffel

The Eiffel Tower is the iconic wrought-iron landmark of **Paris**. Standing at 300 metres, it's the tallest construction in Paris, as tall as an 81-storey building. It took twenty-two months to build.

Duomo di Milano

The Duomo in **Milan** is a huge cathedral famous for its impressive collection of 4,000 statues, gargoyles and other figures.

Designer Clothes

'Designer' clothes are fashionable, luxury clothing carrying the labels of well-known fashion designers such as Chanel, Dior and Versace. They're usually well-made and VERY expensive.

Fashion Week

Fashion week is a big fashion industry event that usually lasts – you guessed it! – a week, during which fashion designers, brands or 'houses' show their latest collections. These runway shows can effect future fashion trends. That means your favourite pair of shoes were possibly inspired by someone's runway design! A fashion 'house' isn't a building or house you live in. It's a company that designs and sells high-end fashion.

Panettone

Panettone is a sweet bread and fruitcake, originally from Milan. It is usually made and enjoyed for celebrations such as Christmas and New Year!

Next up on your trip is **Gdańsk** and **Málaga**. These historic cities are located in the north of Poland and the south of Spain. There are beautiful old towns with lots to explore, so you'd better get going!

Gdańsk

Málaga

Vivian's danced her **shoes** right off! Can you help her get them back?

1. If there's one thing Gdańsk loves, it's amber! How many amber necklaces can you spot?

_____

2. Spain and Poland are home to some wonderful traditional clothes. Which is featured the most?

Żupan

Mantilla

Flamenco dress

_____

3. Spain is famous for catchy music and dancing. How many musical cats can you spot?

_____

4. If you get hungry, why not stop for some tapas? How many tapas dishes can you find in Málaga?

Gdańsk and Málaga

Gdańsk and Málaga both boast rich heritages – Gdańsk is one of Poland's oldest cities, and Málaga is one of the oldest cities in the world!

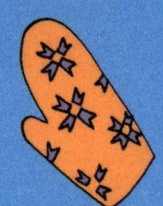

Żupan

The żupan was a long robe worn by men, often made from silk and featuring decorative motifs.

Folk Costumes

Polish folk costumes are regional outfits that are rich in detail and are different from one area to another. For example, in the Łowicz region, women wear colourful striped skirts, white blouses and floral scarves. Meanwhile, the Lachy Sądeckie folk costumes feature embroidered applications on jackets and trousers and careful, delicate embroidery on corsets and shirts.

Amber

Gdańsk is the amber capital of the Baltic Sea, as most amber stones wash up along the beaches there. What is amber? It's fossilised (preserved) tree resin or gum, popular for its lovely orange colour.

Mantilla

This is a traditional Spanish lace or silk veil or shawl worn over the head and shoulders. Mantillas are often worn by women during Holy Week (the week leading up to Easter) and at weddings.

Flamenco

Flamenco is a style of entertainment with music and dance. Flamenco uses acoustic guitars, singing, hand claps, heel stamps and castanets. It is danced in traditional Spanish costumes.

You're in **Amsterdam**, the Netherlands' capital. Boats are bobbing along the canal and everywhere you look people are riding colourful bicycles. Can you hear the wooden clogs clacking on the pavement?

1. The Netherlands is home to some of the most famous artists of all time. How many artist copycats can you find?

   _____

2. Amsterdam is in bloom – look at all those tulips! How many different colours are there?

   _____

3. If you've got a sweet tooth, you've come to the right place! Which of these treats can you spot the most of?

   • Stroopwafels
   • Apple tarts
   • Oliebollen (doughnuts)

Vivian took off her **gloves** to pick tulips, but now she can't find them! Where are they?

Amsterdam

Home to Europe's smallest house and the only floating flower market in the world, Amsterdam is the perfect destination for your catwalk around the world. And did you know there are more bikes in Amsterdam than people? (Well, cats, in this book.)

Clogs
Clogs are the iconic shoes of the Netherlands, and people have been wearing them for over 700 years. They're wooden slip-on shoes that are sturdy and – when stuffed with straw – nice and warm.

Tulips
Tulips were brought to the Netherlands in the sixteenth century and have been a symbol for the country ever since. The tulip is seen as a declaration of love, and every colour has a deeper meaning. For example, yellow means happiness and purple means royalty.

Stroopwafel

A stroopwafel is a thin, round waffle biscuit made from two layers of sweet baked dough held together by a caramel filling. You can lay a stroopwafel on top of a hot cup of tea or coffee to soften it before taking a bite into the oozing caramel. Delicious!

Vincent van Gogh

Vincent van Gogh (1853–1890) was born in Groot-Zundert in the Netherlands. Sadly, he suffered from mental health problems and used painting to help express his emotions. He only painted for about ten years, but in that short time he created more than 2,000 artworks, including the very famous *Sunflowers* and *The Starry Night*.

Rembrandt

Rembrandt Harmenszoon van Rijn (1609–1669) was born in Leiden in the Netherlands and is considered the most important painter in Dutch history. He produced an estimated 600 paintings, including *The Anatomy Lesson*, and 1,400 drawings.

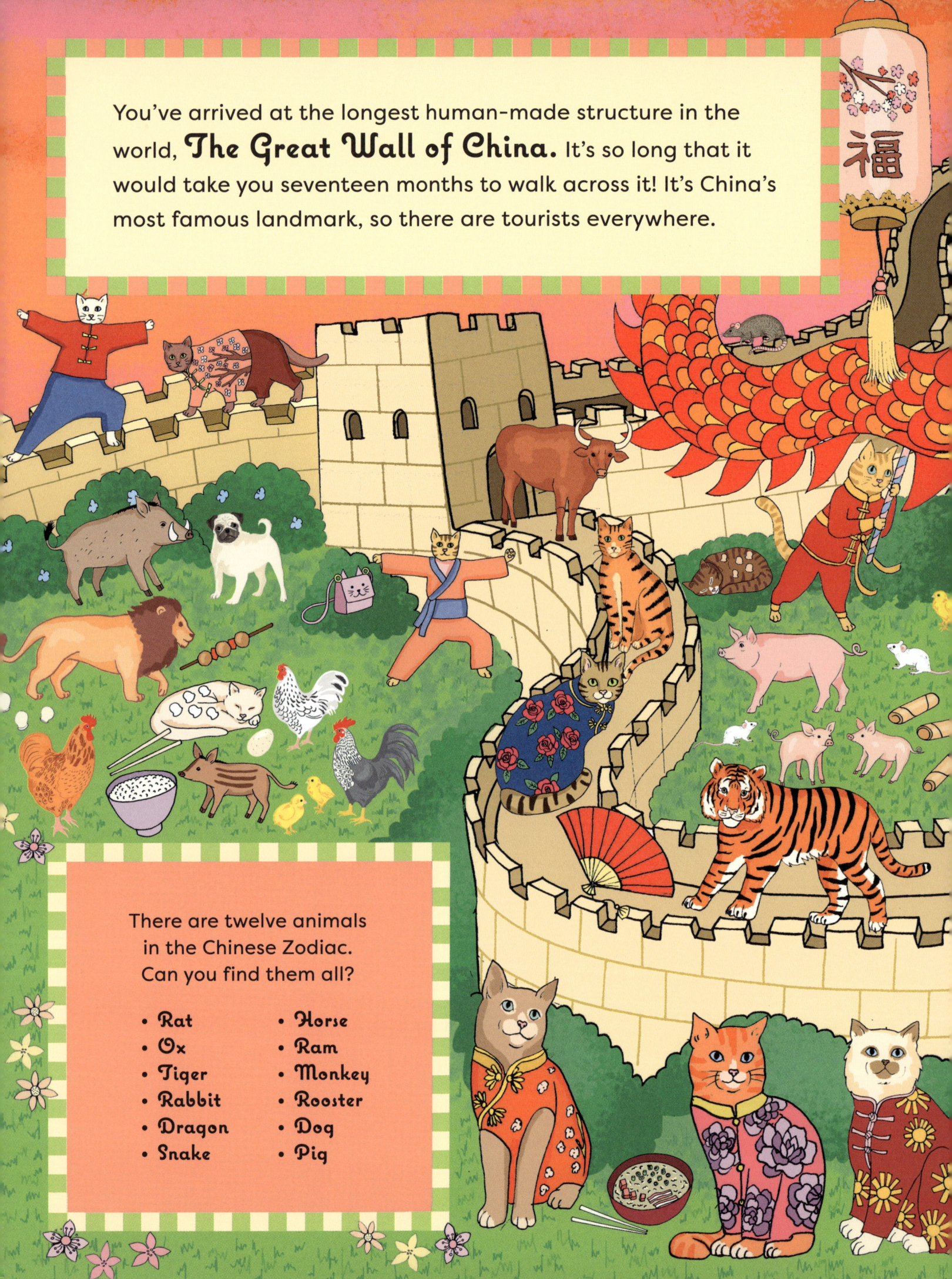

You've arrived at the longest human-made structure in the world, **The Great Wall of China.** It's so long that it would take you seventeen months to walk across it! It's China's most famous landmark, so there are tourists everywhere.

There are twelve animals in the Chinese Zodiac. Can you find them all?

- Rat
- Ox
- Tiger
- Rabbit
- Dragon
- Snake
- Horse
- Ram
- Monkey
- Rooster
- Dog
- Pig

The Great Wall of China

The Great Wall of China is a whopping 21,196 km long and took over 2,000 years to build. Construction of the wall started in 220 BCE and was built for defensive purposes, which is why it's so huge. You can't see it from space, though – that's just a rumour! And the Great Wall is not the only icon of China's rich heritage.

Chèuhngsāam

The chèuhngsāam is a close-fitting silk dress with a high circular collar, side slits and an asymmetrical opening at the front, traditionally secured with knotted buttons and loops. There are different styles of chèuhngsāam in Beijing, Shanghai and Hong Kong, with many differences in the decorations, colours, materials and designs.

Tángzhuāng (Tang Suit)

A Tángzhuāng is a traditional Chinese jacket usually made from silk, brocade or cotton. Originally designed for men, it is now worn by both men and women on special occasions, such as at weddings or at Lunar New Year celebrations.

Chinese Zodiac

Every year represents one of the twelve individual animals of the Chinese Zodiac, which according to legend, raced each other. For example, the year 2000 was the Year of the Dragon. Do you know which animal year were you born on?

Chinese Medicine and Martial Arts

Traditional Chinese medicine has been used for thousands of years and is based on a philosophy of balance with nature.

Chinese cupping is a treatment using heating cups on the skin to increase blood flow to the affected area.

Tai Chi was first developed as a martial art in China, but it is now a popular form of exercise. It involves a series of slow gentle movements performed with controlled breathing. It is very relaxing!

Tai chi

Cupping

Kon'nichiwa (hello), and welcome to **Tokyo.** With both traditional shrines and high-tech robots, Japan's capital is the perfect blend of traditional and modern. Take it all in!

Vivian's bought a flower chain in an outdoor market, but she's dropped her old **necklace**. Better find it before you have to say sayōnara (goodbye)!

Tokyo

Tokyo is a fast-paced city famous for incredible fashion, anime, electronics and vending machines that sell everything from hamburgers to umbrellas! It's home to one of the busiest pedestrian crossings in the world, Shibuya Crossing, which sees a staggering average of 300,000 crossers every day.

Kimono

Kimonos have been worn for over a thousand years and are the national dress of Japan. They have square sleeves and a rectangular body and are traditionally worn with a broad sash called an obi and accessories such as zōri sandals and tabi socks.

Yukata

A yukata is another type of traditional robe, similar to the kimono. 'Yukata' literally means 'bathing cloth' — it was traditionally worn after a dip in a communal bath or an onsen (hot spring).

Harajuku Street Style

As well as being one-of-a-kind, colourful and fun, Harajuku fashion celebrates community and freedom of expression.

Mochi

Mochi is a Japanese dessert made of sweet glutinous (sticky) rice flour. Mochi dough is often tinted with matcha (green tea powder) or other food colourings and wrapped around a sweet centre. This delicious bite-sized dessert has a chewy, smooth and elastic texture.

Cherry Blossom

The blossom of the cherry tree is known as sakura in Japanese. It symbolises the return of spring, as well as renewal and hope. The perfect pink petals only bloom for about a week, so see them while you can!

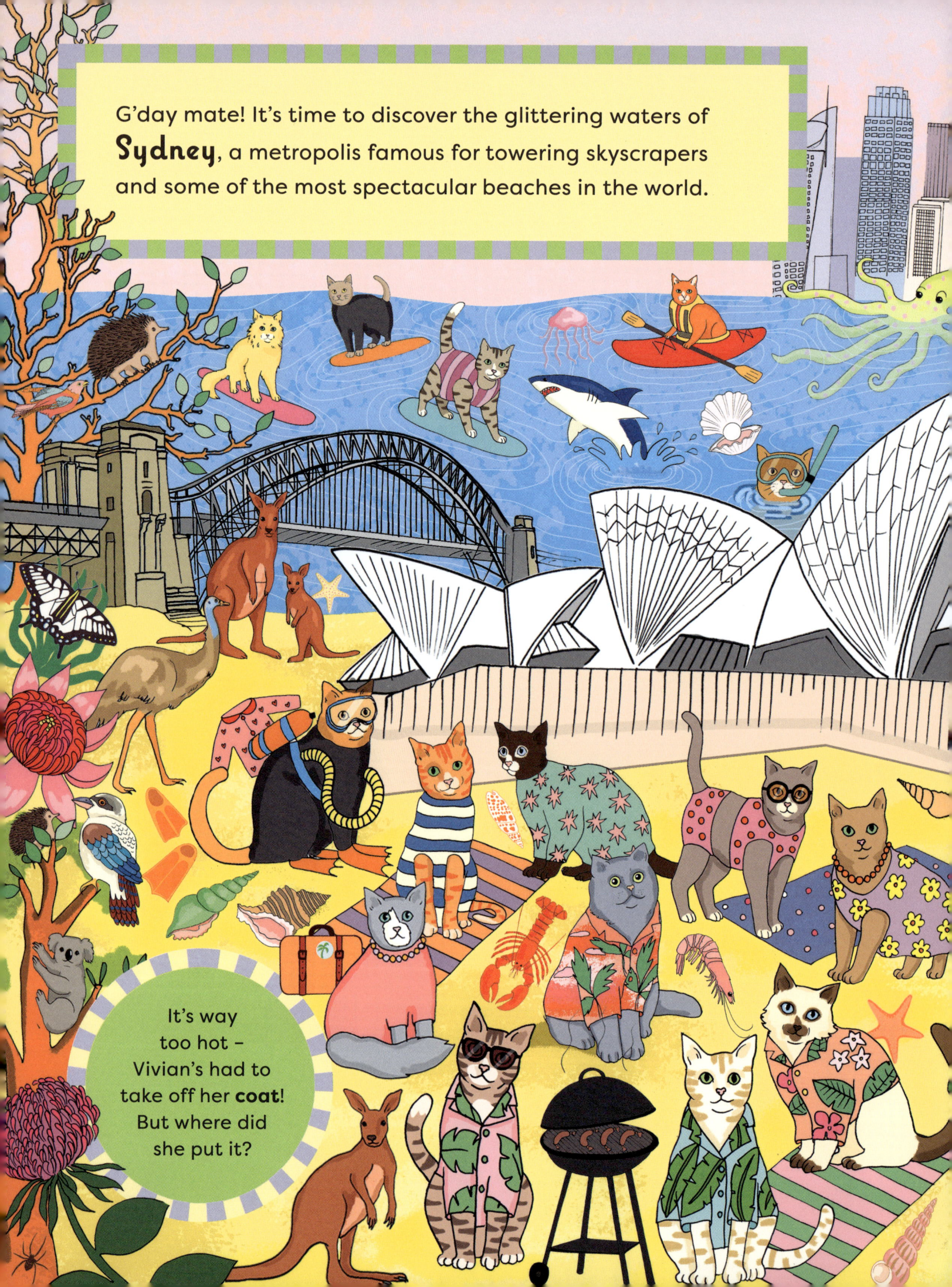

Sydney

Sydney officially became a city in 1842. Despite what a lot of people think, Sydney's not the capital city of Australia – that would be Canberra. With the Blue Mountains in the distance, and its incredible beaches, it's no surprise that Sydney is a hugely popular tourist spot.

The Sydney Opera House

The Sydney Opera House is one of the world's most famous buildings and Australia's most recognisable human-made landmark. It was opened by Queen Elizabeth II in 1973 and is so big that about 15,500 light bulbs must be changed there every year. Just imagine the electricity bill!

Harbour Bridge

The Sydney Harbour Bridge is tallest steel arch bridge in the world, standing at 134 metres from top to water level. It's nicknamed 'the coat hanger' because of its arch-based design, but you'd struggle to hang your clothes on something so tall.

Australian Animals

Most of Australia's animals are endemic, which means they are found nowhere else in the world. Platypuses, wombats, emus and Tasmanian devils are some of the many animals that you can only find in Australia. Did you find the other endemic animals on the previous spread?

Wombat

Emu

Platypus

Tasmanian devil

Australian Plants

There are many endemic plants in Australia too. The red-pink gum tree is a favourite of koalas and the furry kangaroo paw is named for its velvety flowers that look like — you guessed it! — kangaroo paws.

Gum tree

Kangaroo paw

Welcome to the city that never sleeps – **New York** – the perfect destination to end your catwalk around the world! Your senses are in overdrive – you can smell the pizza, hear the busy traffic and see so many dazzling city lights. Where to begin?

1. Theatre enthusiasts love New York for one reason – Broadway! How many wonderful Broadway cat spin-off shows can you spot?

2. New York never sleeps so it's important to keep your energy up. Let's go for a pizza! How many slices of pizza can you spot in this scene?

3. It's been a great trip, but it's time to head home. Hail down the yellow cab without a passenger. Hey – **taxi!**

New York

With lots of culture and entertainment to offer, and home to approximately 8.5 million people, the Big Apple is one of the most exciting cities to visit in the USA — and the world!

Broadway

The best New York shows, from up-and-coming plays to big and bold musicals, take place in the over forty professional theatres in the Broadway district. Broadway itself has some longstanding superstitions, from breaking a leg (which actually means good luck), to not whistling in a theatre, to the use of a ghost light to ward off spirits. Spooky!

The Empire State Building

Once the tallest building in the world, the Empire State Building was built in 1931. Its art deco design is thought to have been based on the humble pencil, and with up to 3,400 workers teaming up on its construction every day, it only took twenty months to complete.

The Statue of Liberty

'Lady Liberty' was a present from France to the American people as a monument to American freedom. The statue, which stands at 46 metres and 2.5 centimetres, sways in the wind, so be careful climbing her on a blustery day!

Film and TV

As it's such a dynamic, interesting city, with a huge variety of people, landmarks and neighbourhoods, New York is the setting of many beloved movies and TV shows. So if the city looks familiar to you, that might be why!

New York Cabs

An entrepreneur, Harry N. Allen, started the New York Taxicab Company in 1907 to compete with very high fares for the horse-drawn carriages on the streets of New York. He imported sixty-five cars from France and painted them a distinguishable yellow.

Answers

Scotland
1. Kilts — five cats are wearing them. Tweed: three cats; Tam o' Shanter cap: two cats.
2. Eight — shortbread; porridge; Empire biscuit; fish and chips; cranachan; haggis, neeps and tatties; tea cake, scotch egg.
3. Three highland cows, one Loch Ness monster, three puffins.
4. *To a Mouse* — four copies. *A Red, Red Rose*: three copies; *Auld Lang Syne*: two copies.

Paris and Milan
1. Quilted bags: four; Pearl necklaces: seven; Chunky gold chains: three; Spiky shoes: two.
2. Croissants: four; eclairs: four; gelato: five; pasta: eleven.

Gdańsk and Málaga
1. Eighteen amber necklaces.
2. Flamenco Dresses — eight cats are wearing them. Żupan: two cats; mantilla: three cats.
3. Seven musical cats.
4. Thirteen dishes — churros, olives, tortilla, cured ham, padrón peppers, croquettes, paella, prawn tapa, Spanish crostini, cheese tapa, chorizo and cured ham tapa.

Amsterdam
1. Three copycat artists — Rembrandt, van Gogh and Vermeer.
2. Six colours of tulips — red, orange, yellow, pink, purple and white.
3. Stroopwafel — there are fourteen. Apple tarts: four; oliebollen: thirteen.

China
1. Tai Chi: six cats; cupping: five cats.
2. Seven — congee, chuan meat skewer, sticky rice, spring rolls, wontons, chow mein and wonton soup.

Tokyo
1. Kimono — ten cats are wearing them. Harajuku: 5 cats.
2. Five types of flower — cherry blossom, golden-rayed lily, lotus flower, violets and camellia.

Sydney
1. Canoeing; surfing; snorkelling; scuba diving
2. Koala: four; kangaroo: four; echidna: five
3. Waratah has the most — six. Gum tree: five; eucalyptus: three.

New York
1. There are seven — *Wicked, Cats, Frozen, The Sound of Music, The Lion King, The Phantom of the Opera* and *Elvis: The Musical*.
2. Eight slices of pizza.